Relaxing Places

An Adult Coloring Book

by

C.C. Shepard

info@ccshepardart.com

ISBN-10:0-9983346-0-X
ISBN-13:978-0-9983346-0-8

Front cover: "Beach #2" colored by: Lindsey Ravinski

Back cover: "Four Season Porch" colored by: Ailee Ravinski, age 5
"Graveyard" colored by: Jessica Tyson
"Dining Room" colored by: Stephanie Weller
"Chair and Table" colored by: Kirsten Aune
"Beach #2" colored by: Melissa Weisser
"Woman In Garden" colored by: Kirsten Aune

Special thanks to family and friends for their help and support.

INTRODUCTION

It had been years, but 2015 found me drawing again. I was fortunate to travel and experience peaceful, relaxing places. Equipped with a new sketchbook and a black marker, I would pick out a scene and sit down. With my hands out in front of my eyes, I'd frame the view and start drawing the closest thing to me. Each sketch took 30 to 60 minutes.

   In the back of this book you'll find information about each drawing. You can decide to read the details first or just start coloring without knowing where, or what time of day they were drawn. It's up to you. Put the sun or moon anywhere you want.

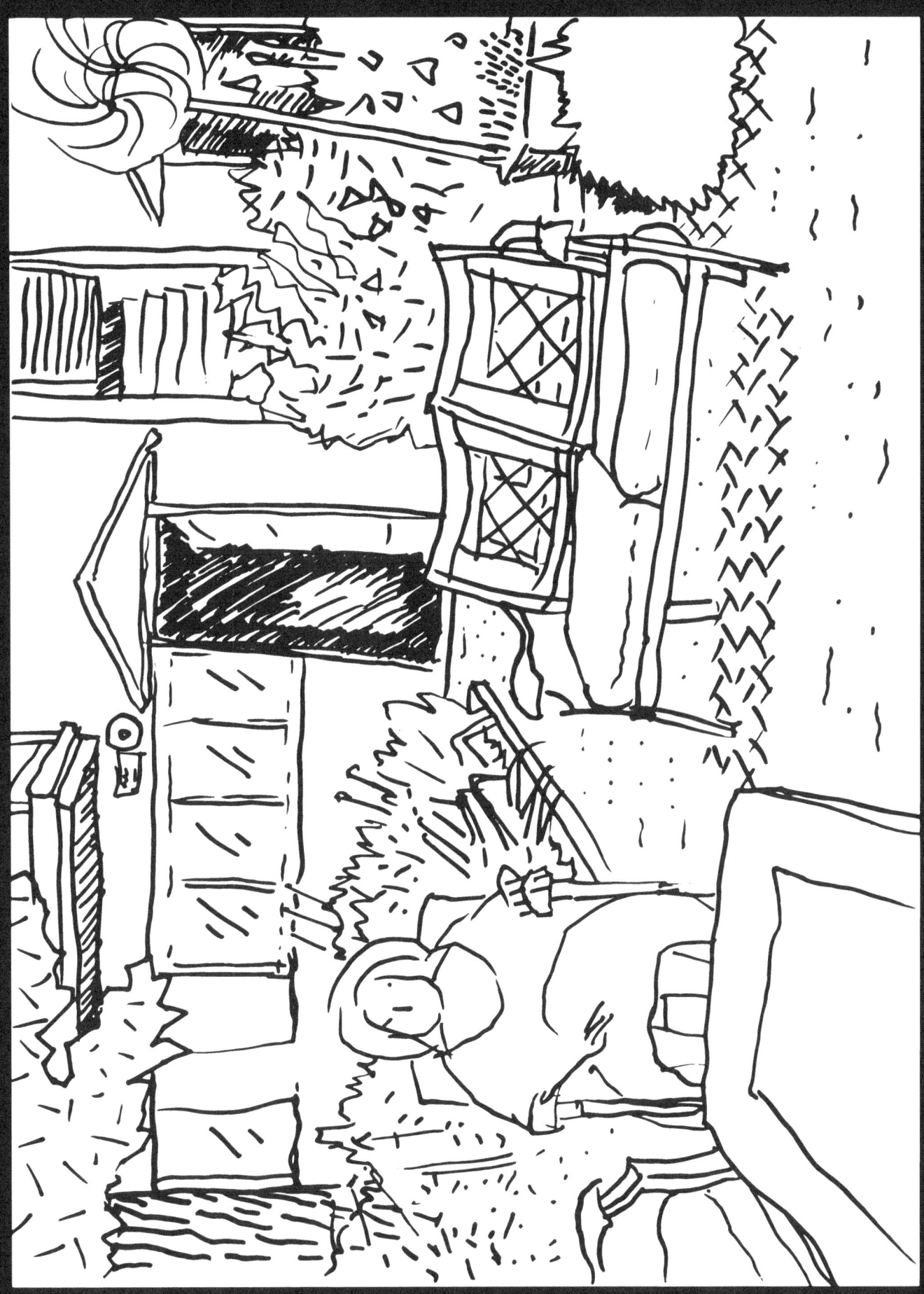

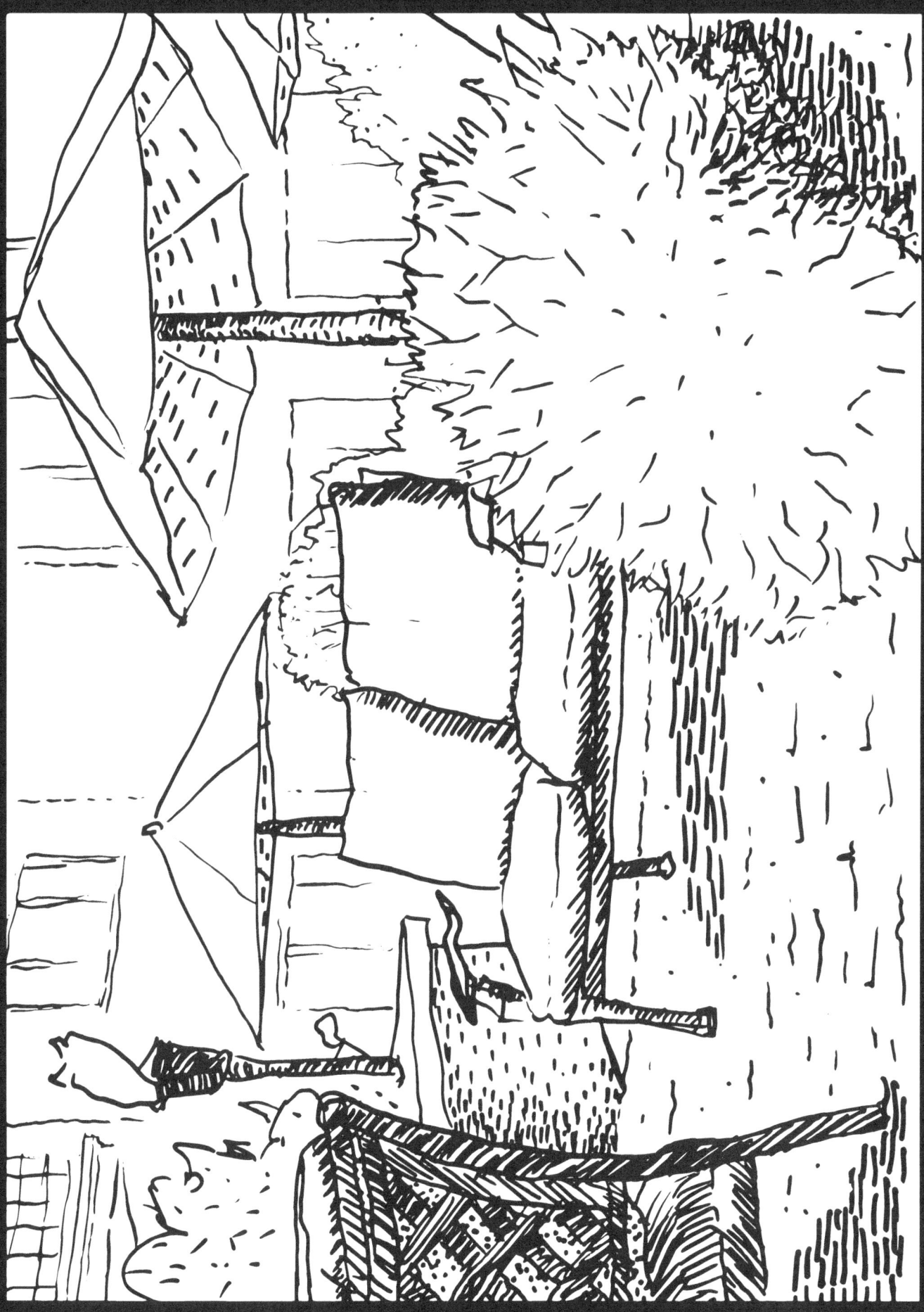

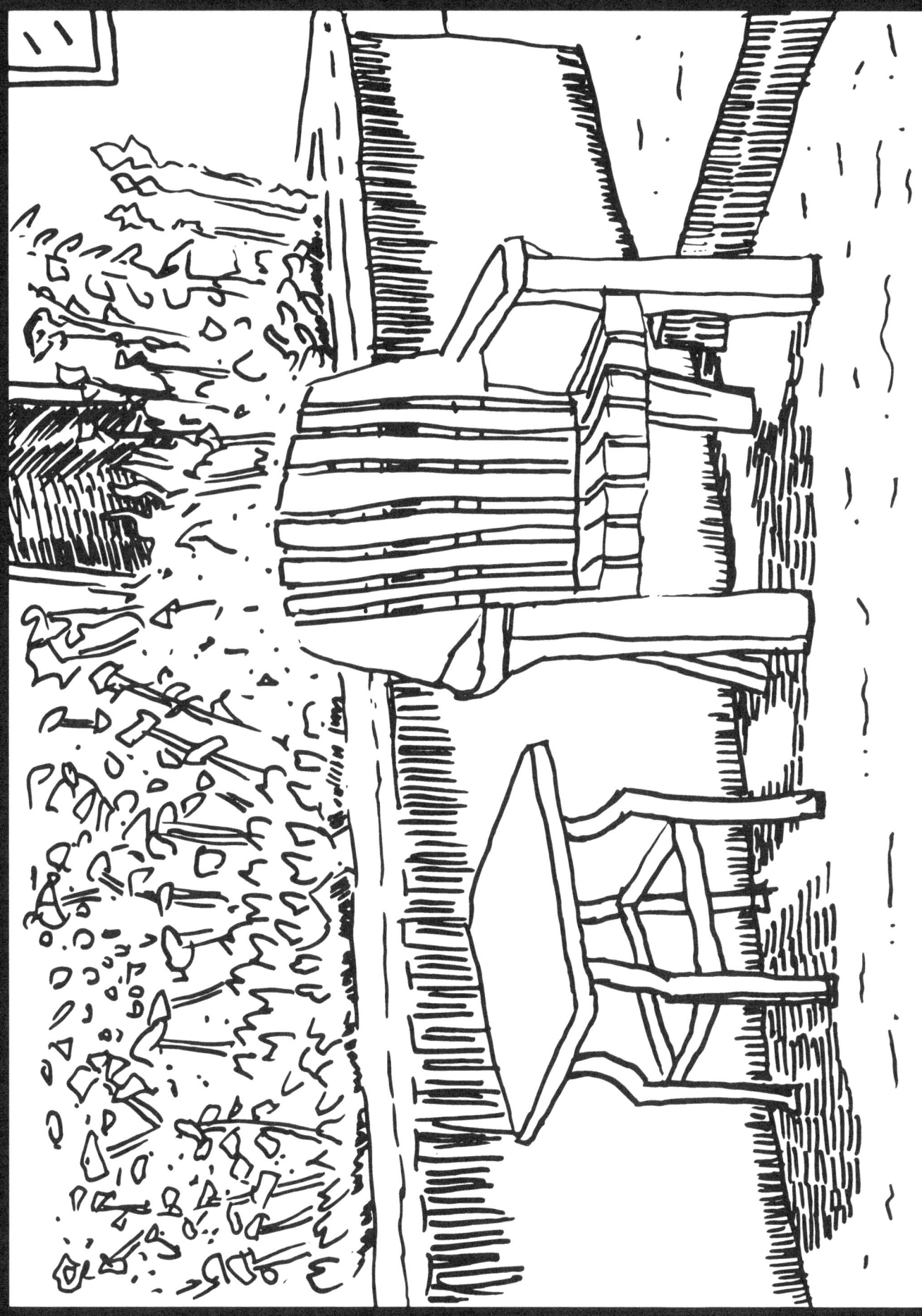

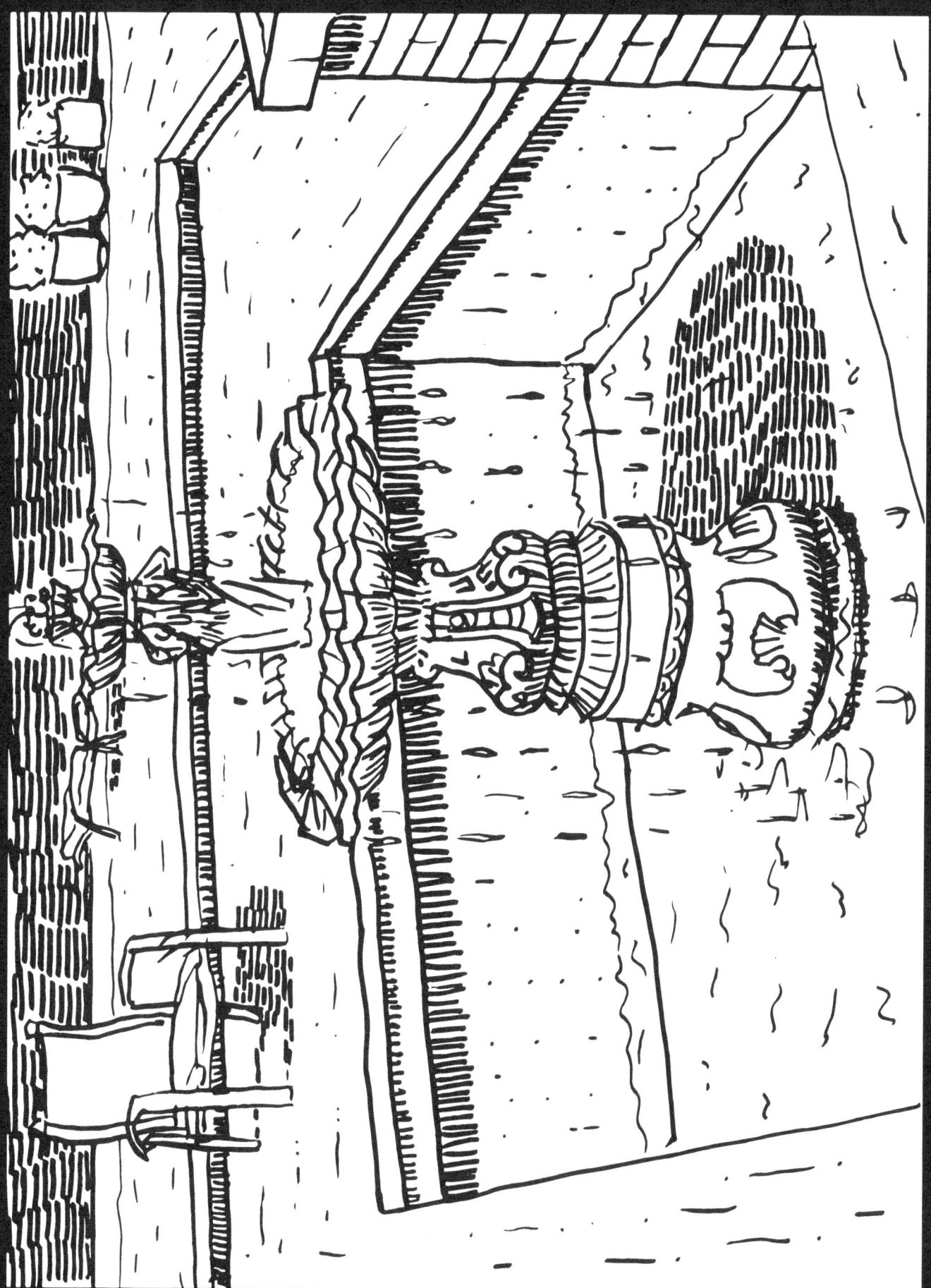

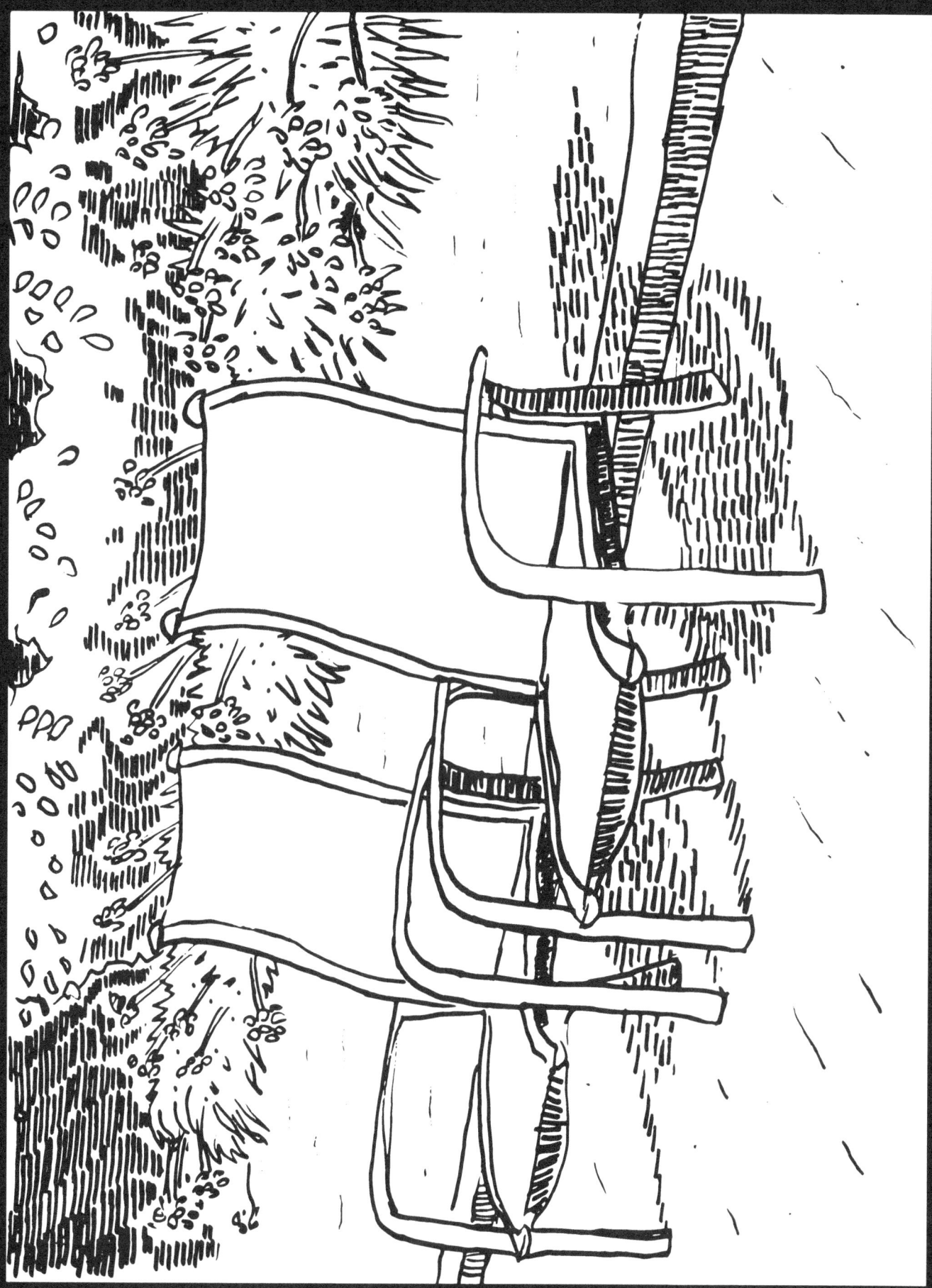

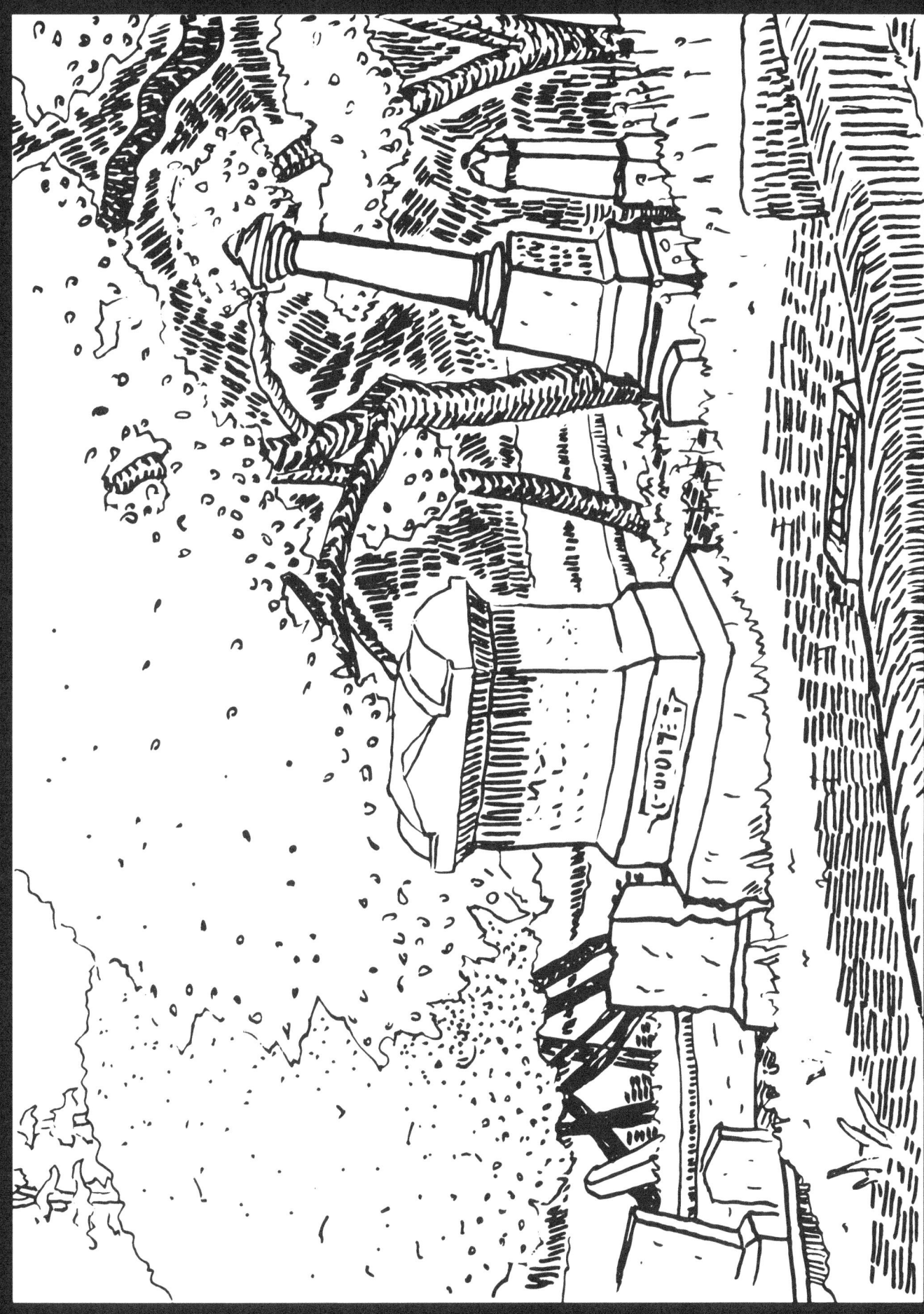

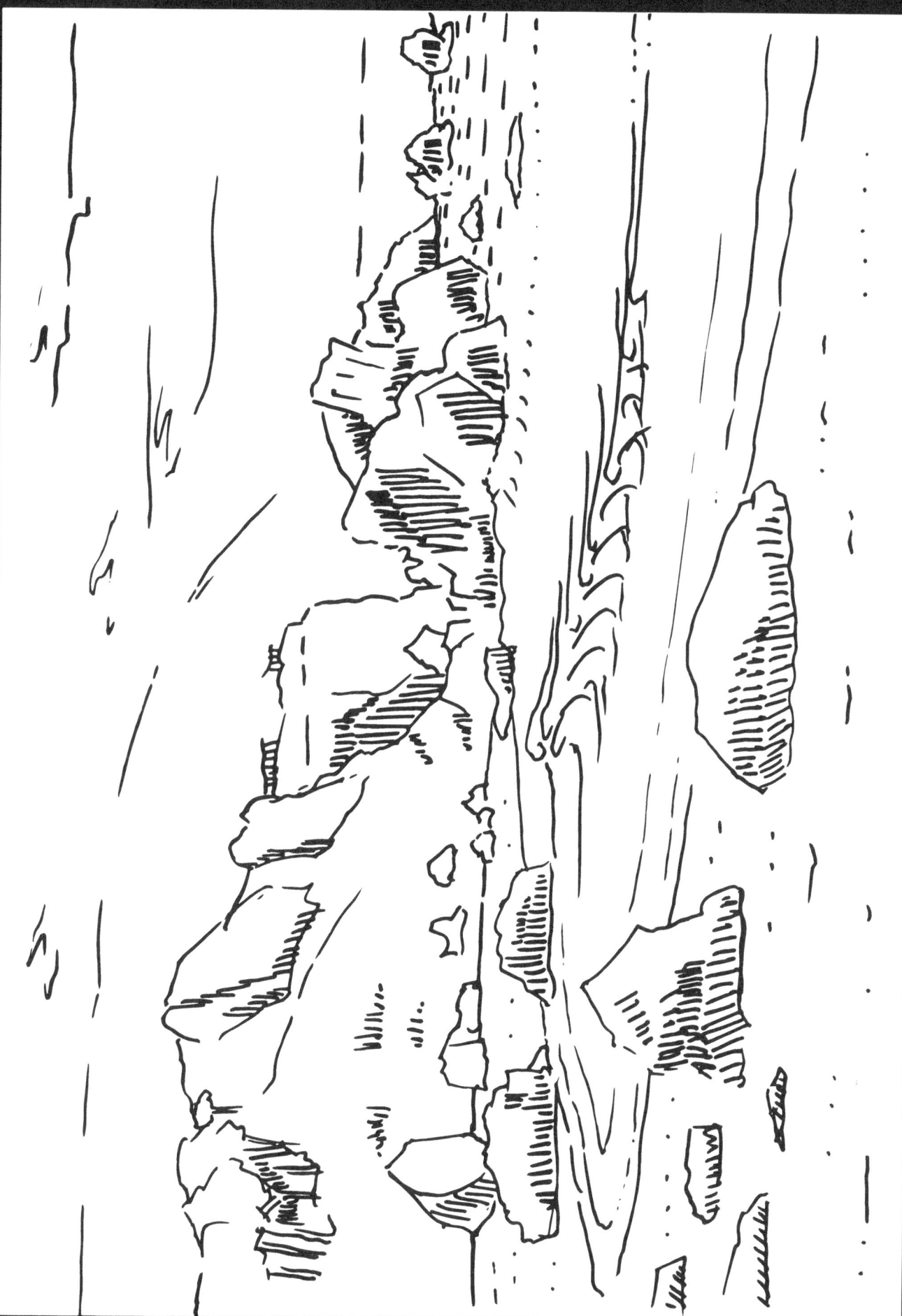

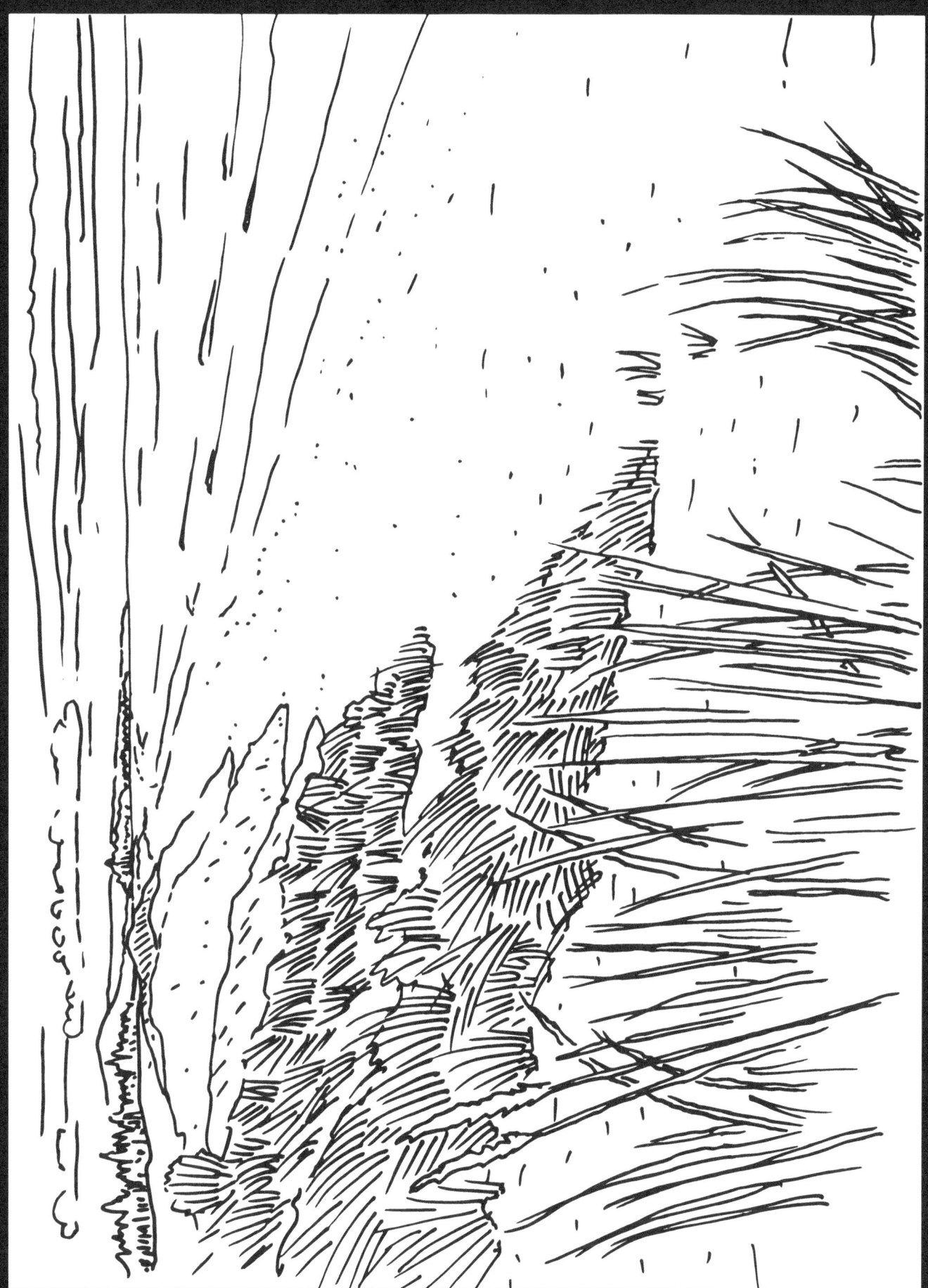

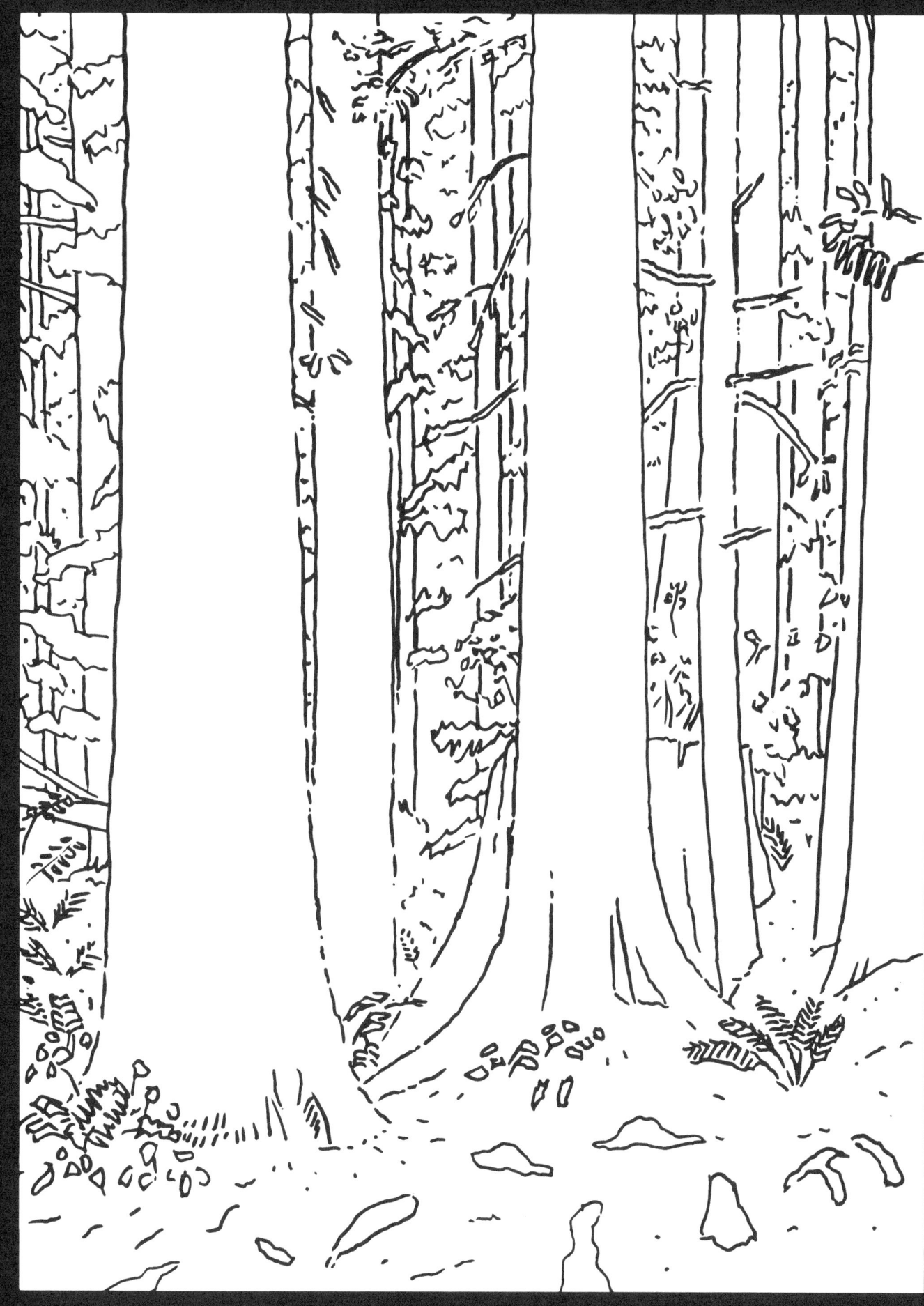

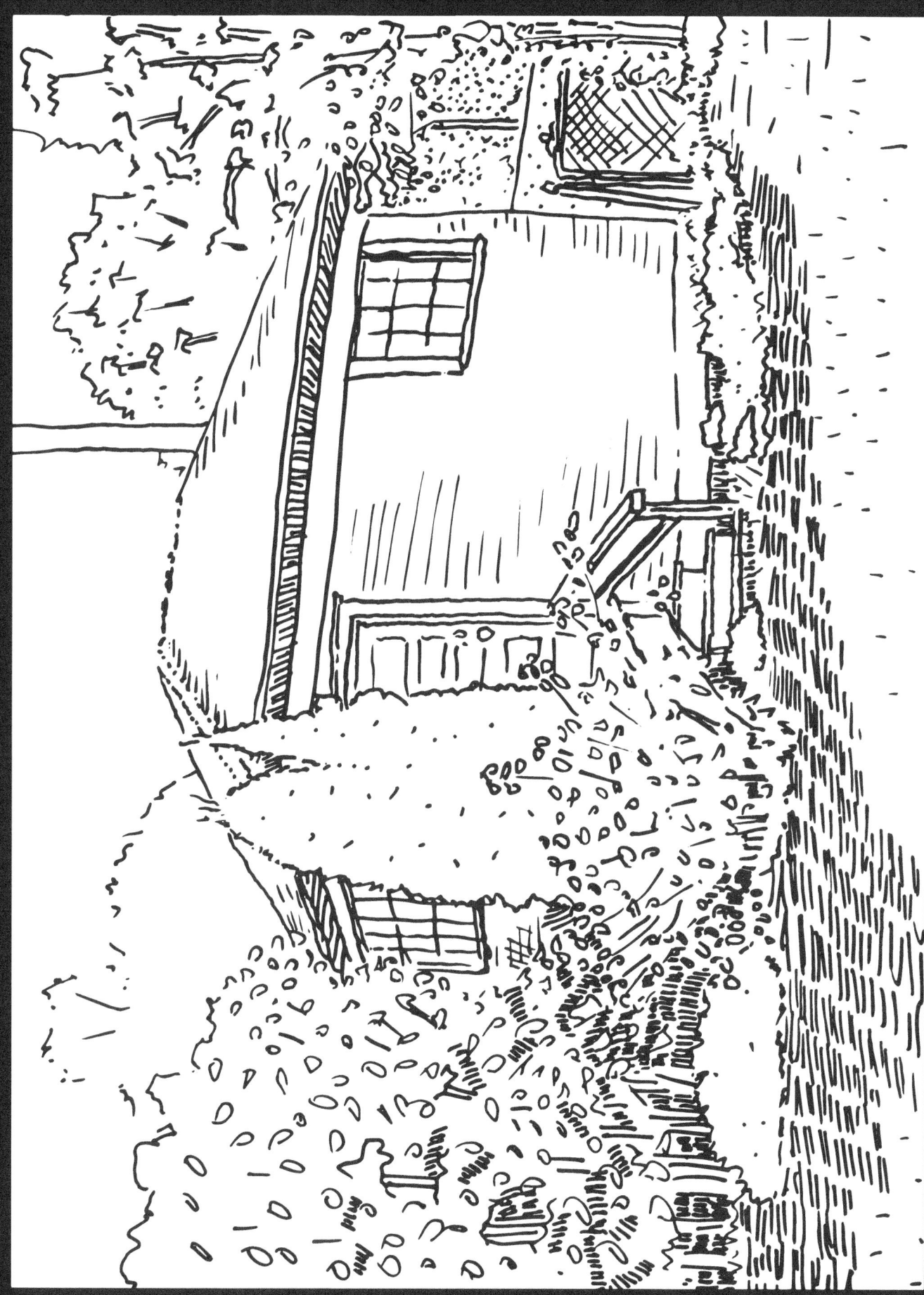

Test Page

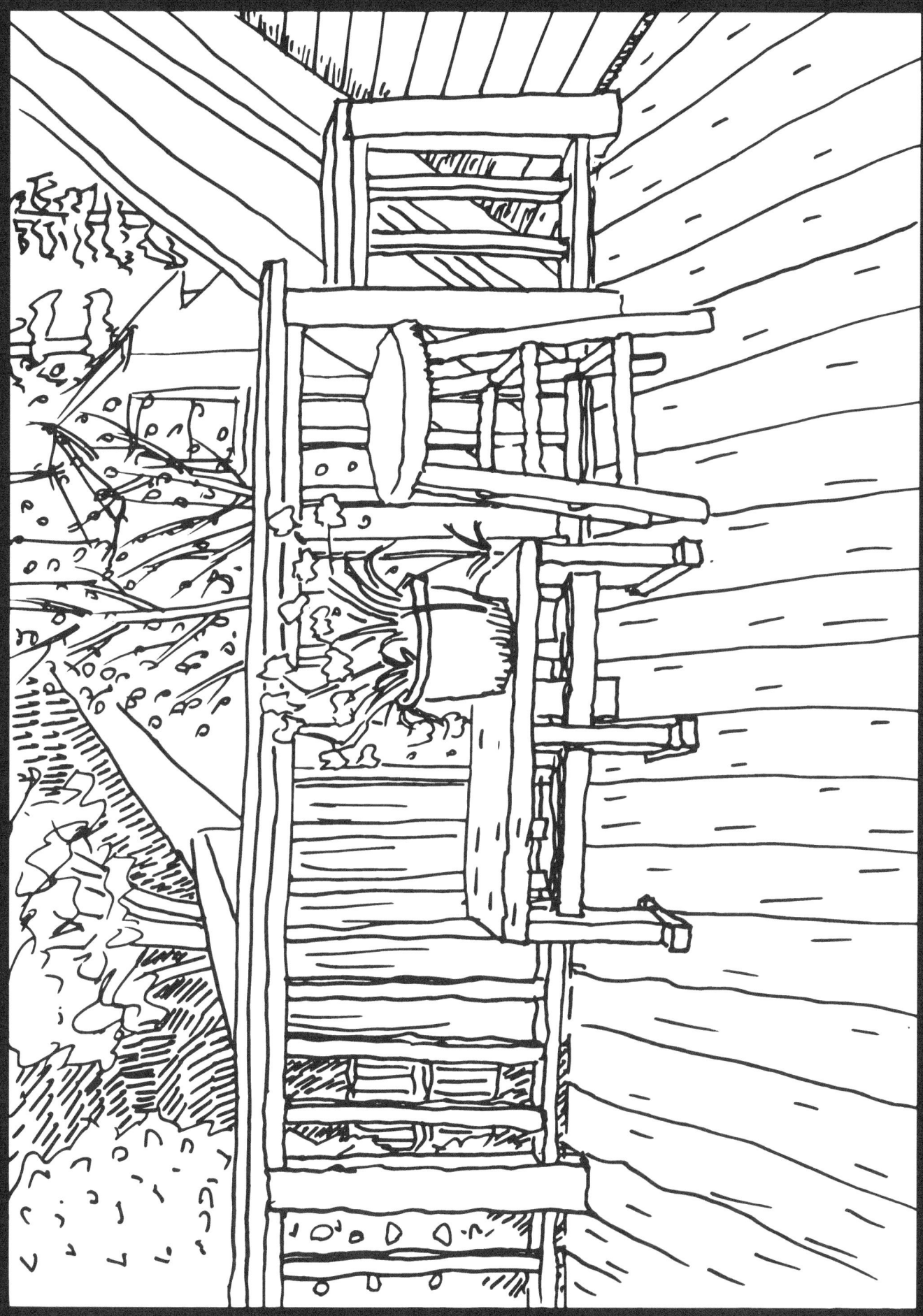

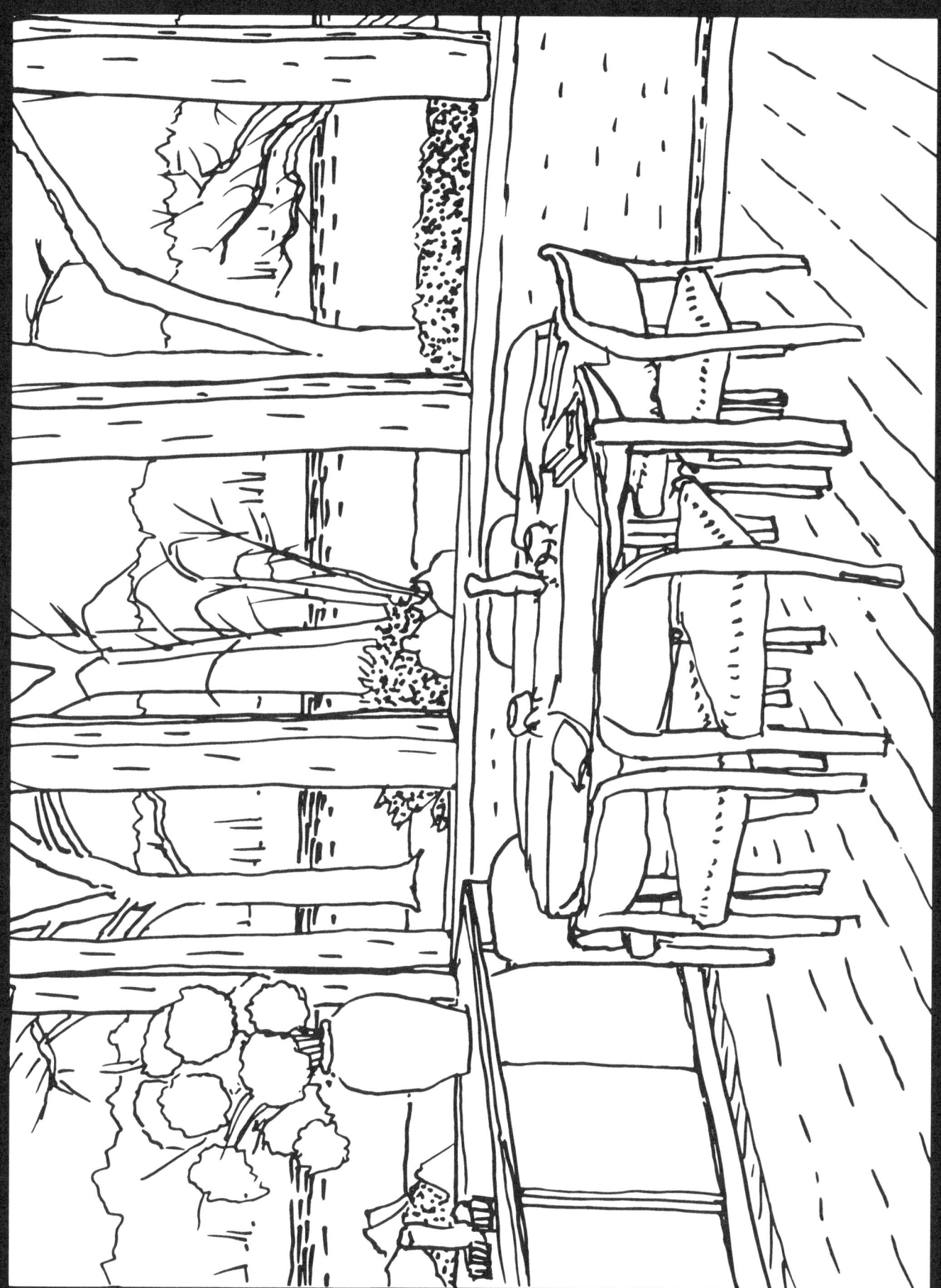

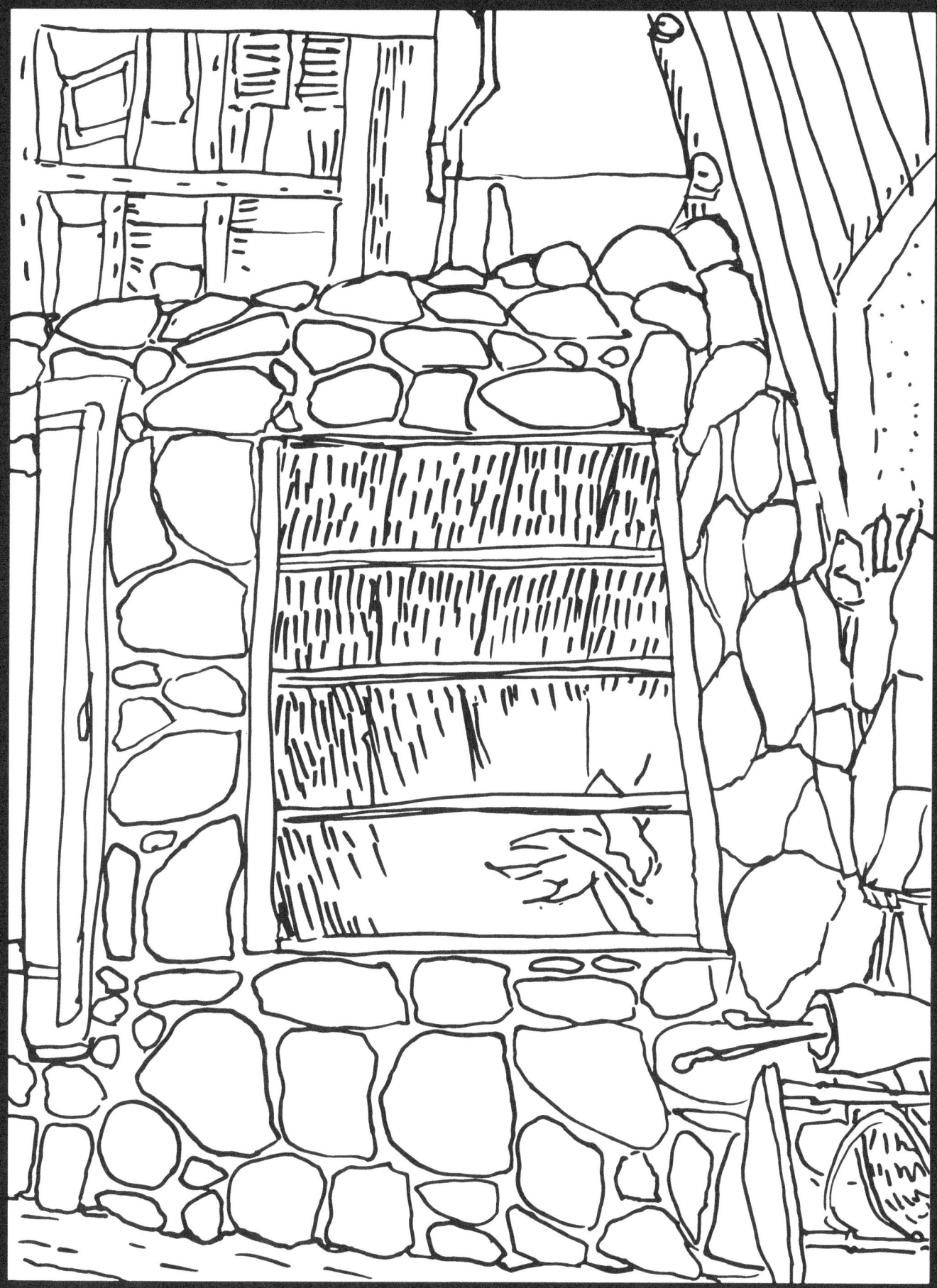

Test Page

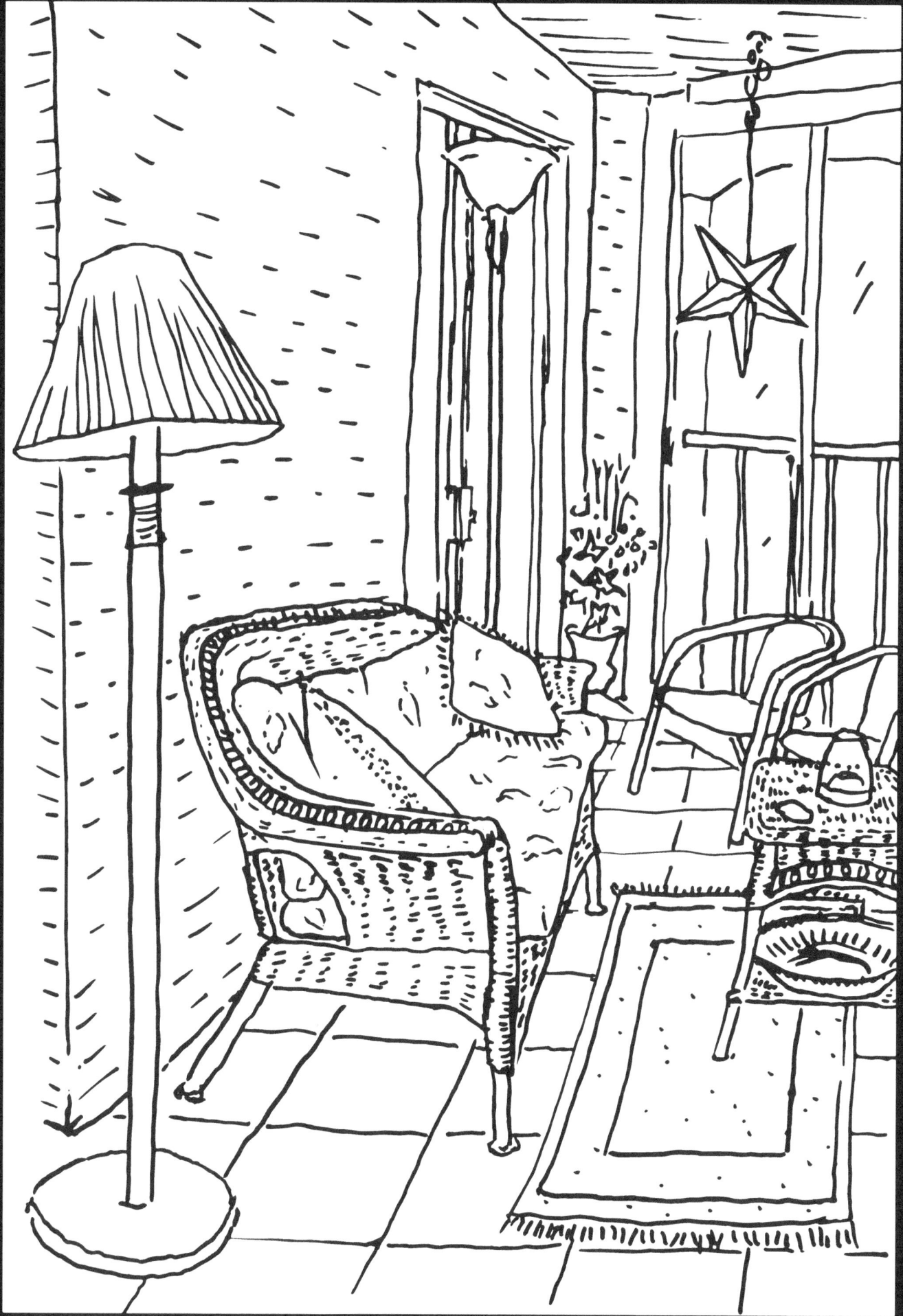

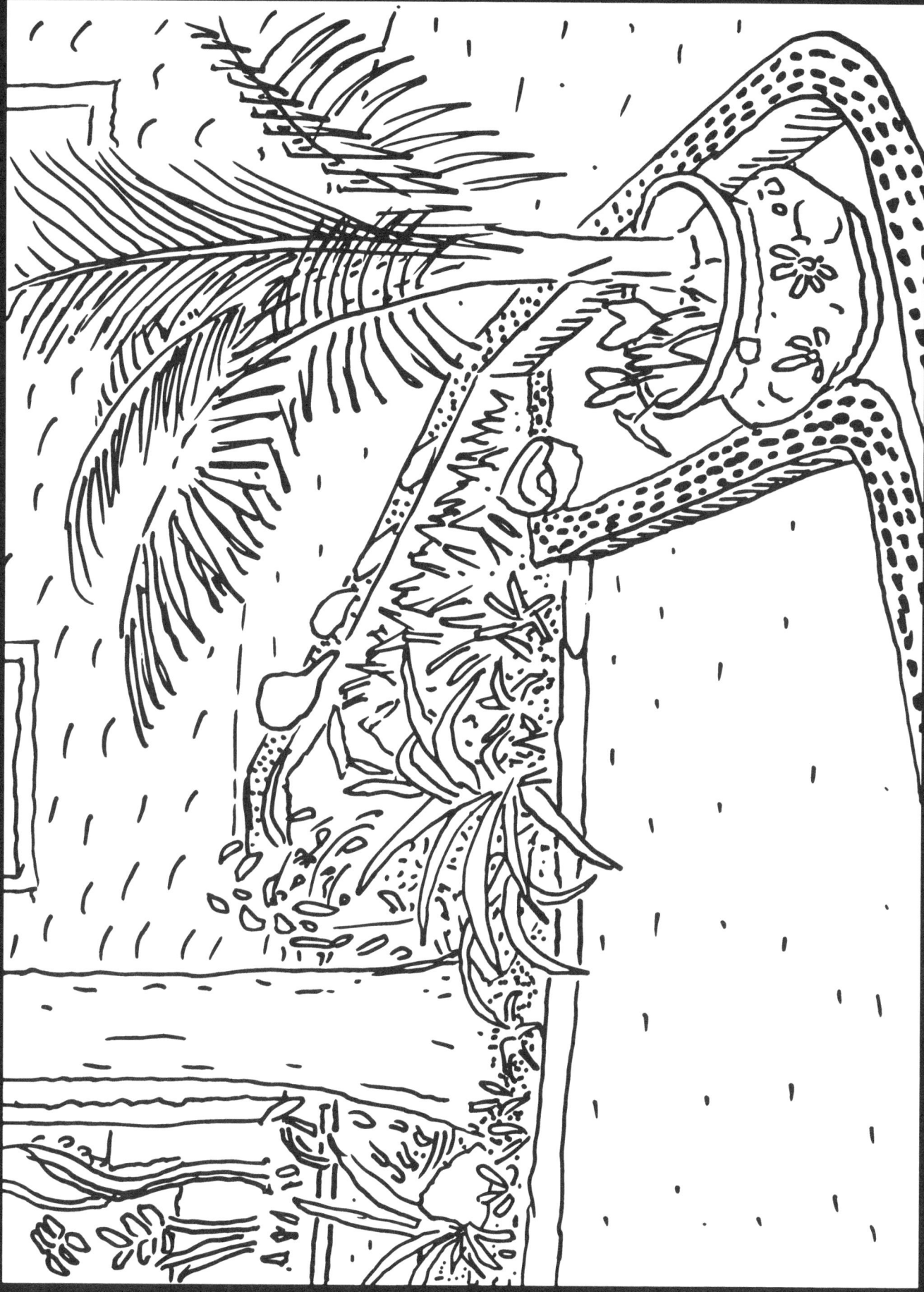

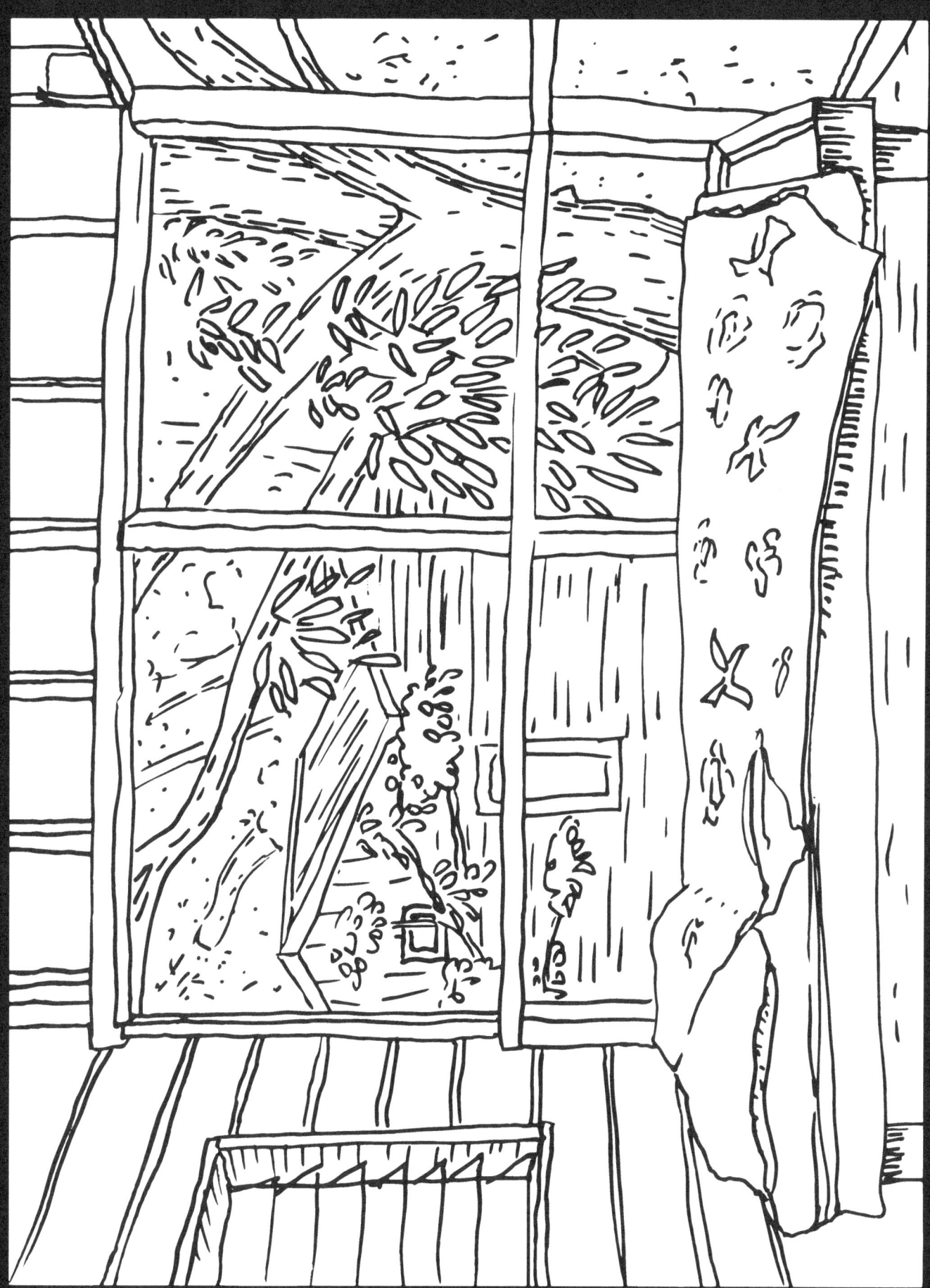

Test Page

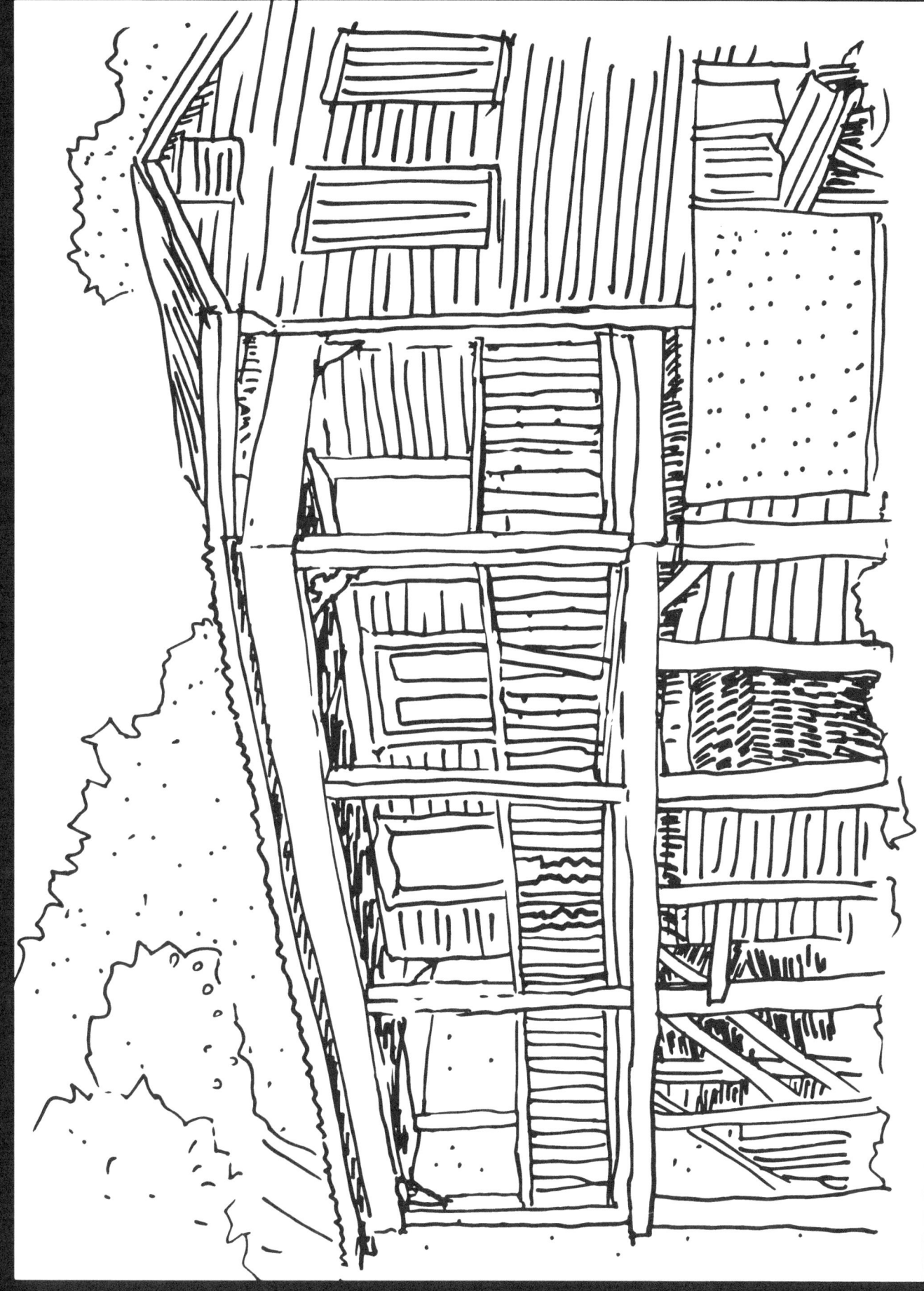

Test Page

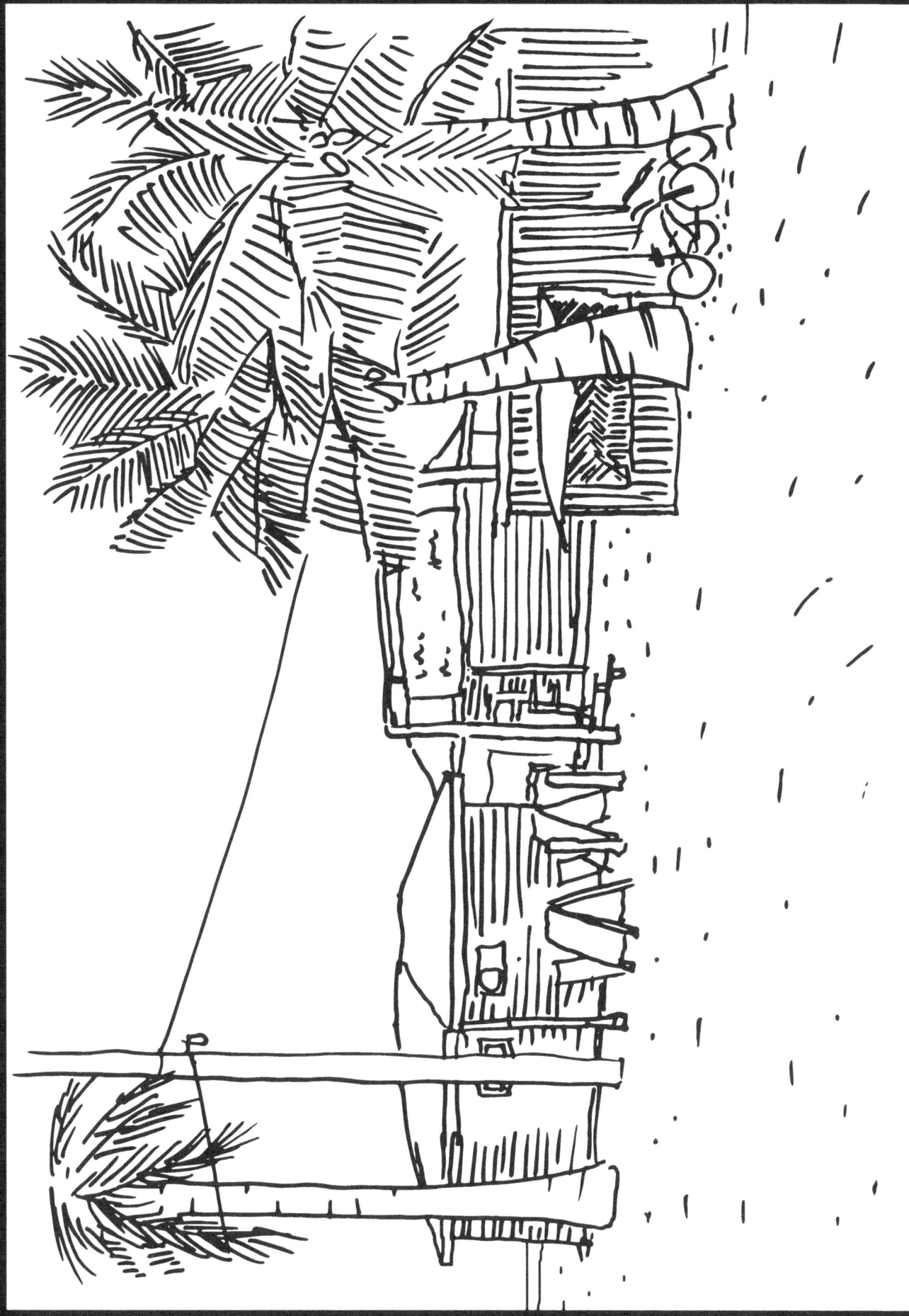

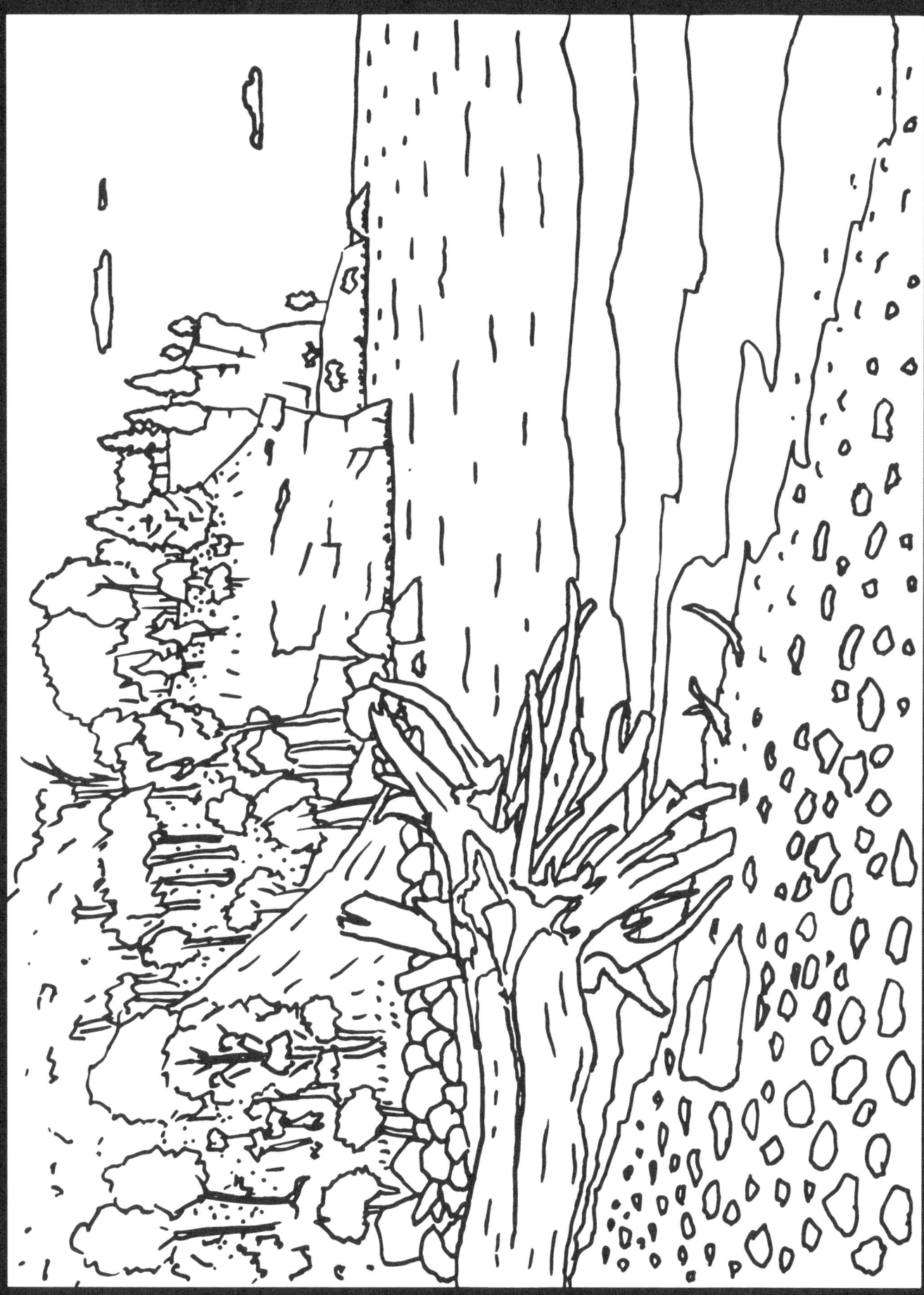

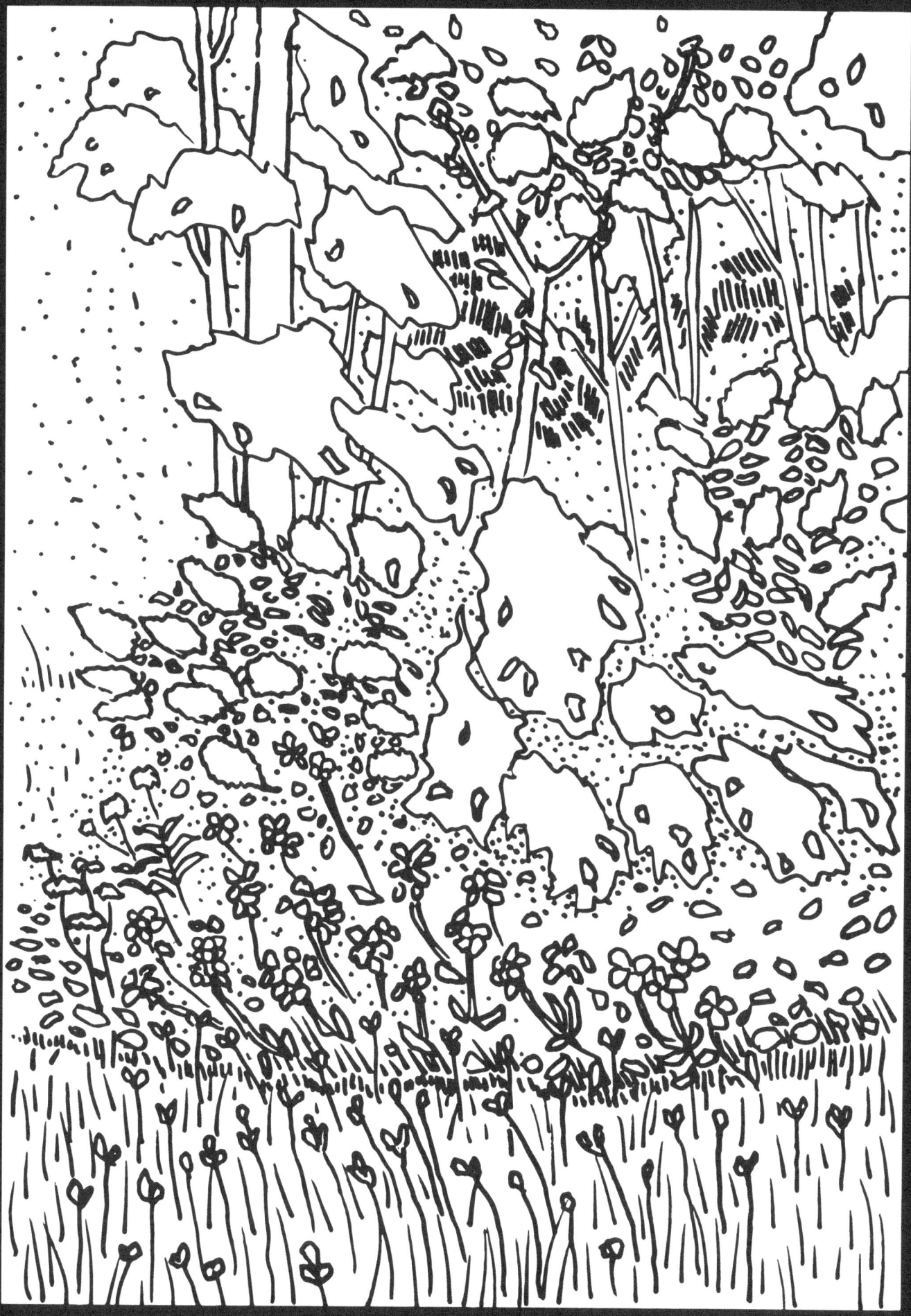

Test Page

APPENDIX

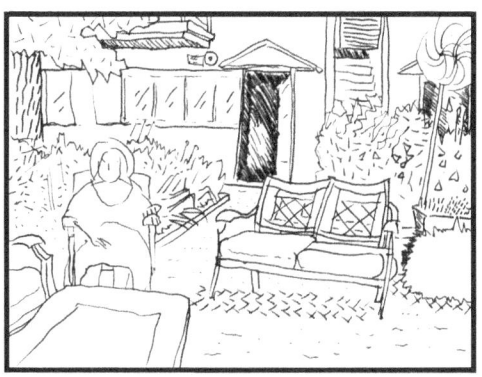

"Woman in Garden" p. 5
Santa Rita, California
July, 2015, midday, sunny.
The first sketch for this series. It was not my
intention to draw people. I wanted to concentrate
on landscapes, but halfway through the drawing,
a woman walked into the scene and sat down.
Well, there she is.

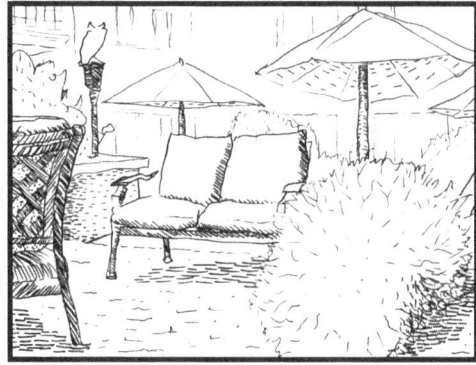

"Patio" p.9
Santa Rita, California
July, midday, sunny.

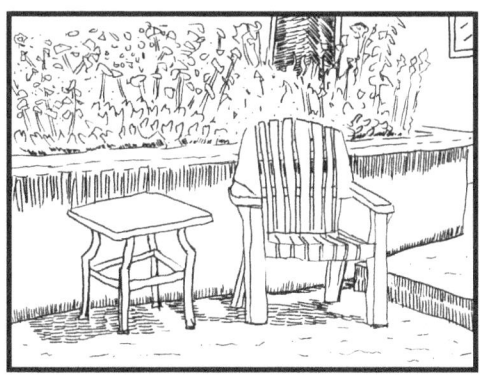

"Chair and Table" p. 13
Santa Rita, California
July, midday, sunny.

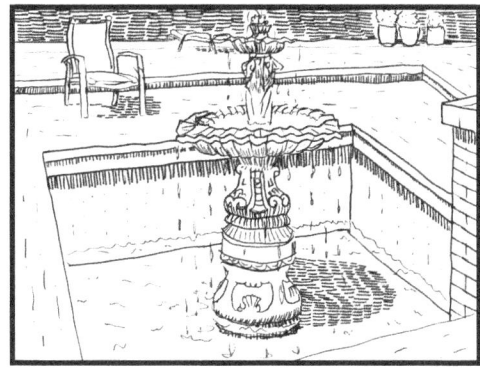

"Fountain" p. 17
Santa Rita, California
July, midday, sunny.

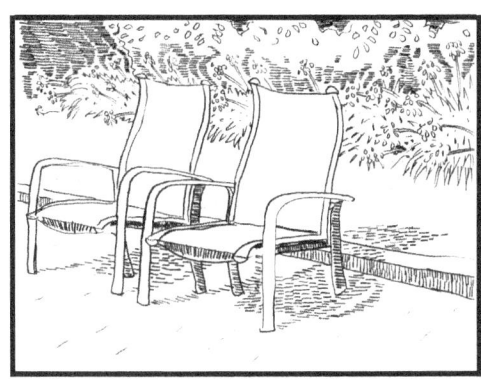

"Two Chairs" p. 21
Santa Rita, California
July, midday, sunny.

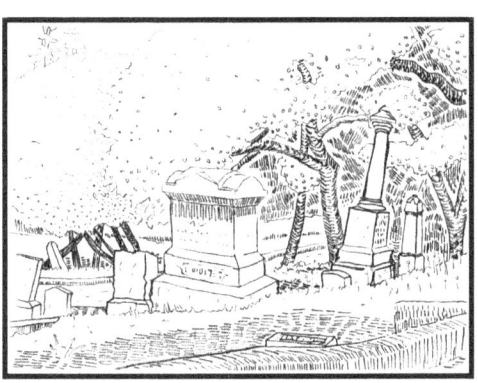

"Graveyard" p. 25
Santa Rita, California
July, early afternoon, sunny.
It was very hot. I found a nice place to sit in
the shade. All was quiet except for a couple of
hummingbirds checking me out from a nearby
branch.

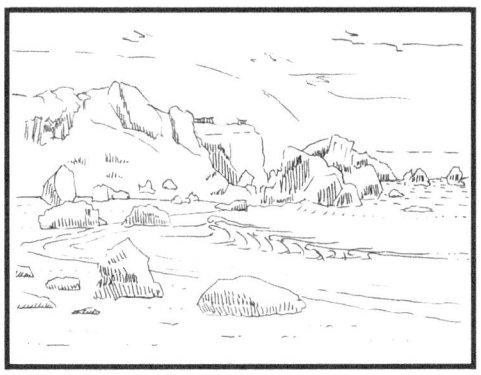

"Beach #1" p. 29
A few miles north of Arcata, California
August, afternoon, partly cloudy with fog.
People were swimming. Pelicans were feeding
and a big dungeness crab crawled out of the surf.
Surrounded by fog and clouds, the sun somehow
managed to shine through.

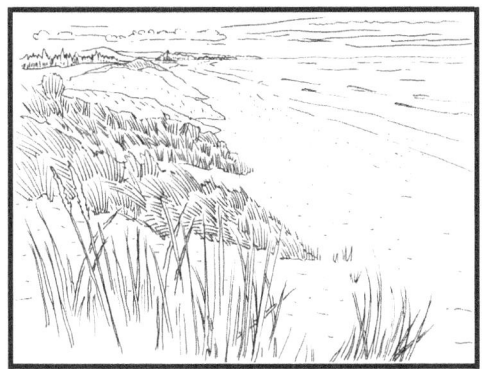

"Beach #2" p. 33
Mad River County Park north of Arcata, California
August, afternoon, overcast.

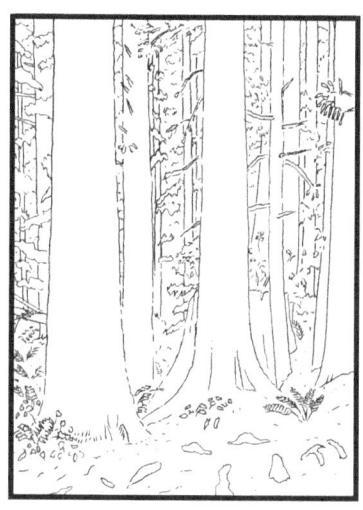

"Redwoods" p. 37
Humboldt State University, Arcata, California
August, afternoon, sunny but well shaded.
A second growth redwood forest. Evidence of old growth is the stump behind two trees whose diameter is quite awesome. This was drawn while sitting at the picnic table beside the first tee of the Redwood Curtain Disc Golf Course.

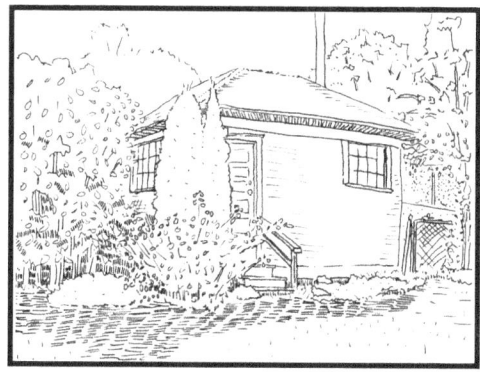

"Garage" p. 41
Duluth, Minnesota
September, late afternoon, sunny.

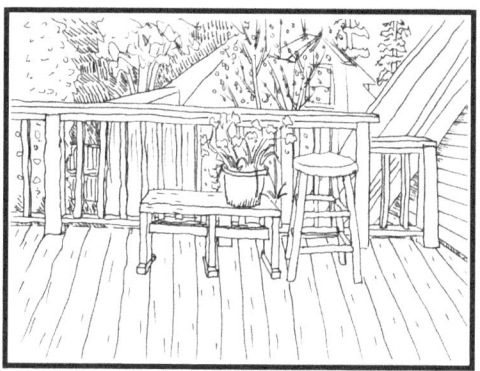

"Deck" p. 45
Duluth, Minnesota
October, early evening, overcast.
Fall colors are in full swing. It's cold and dusk is descending.

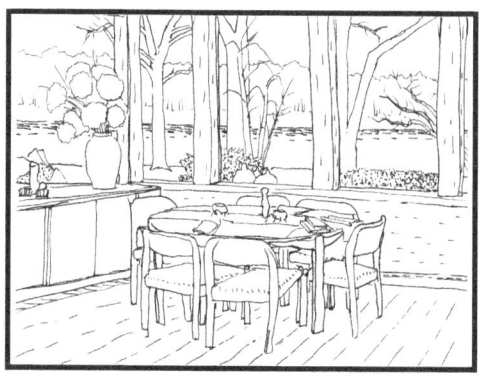

"Dining Room" p. 49
Sartell, Minnesota
November, midday, overcast.
Looking out on the Mississippi River.

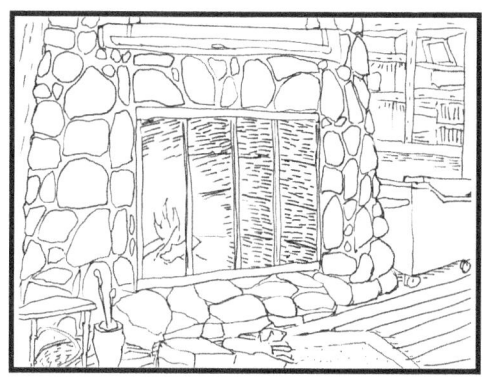

"Fireplace" p. 53
Southern Minnesota
December, late afternoon.

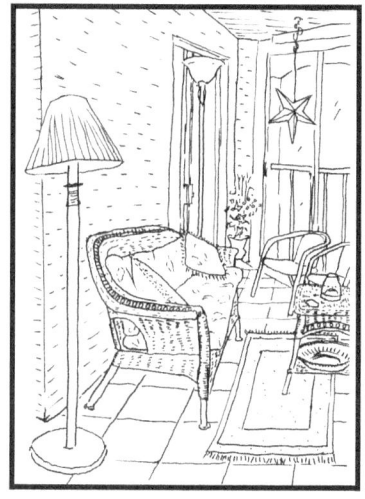

"Four Season Porch", p. 57
Minneapolis, Minnesota
December, midday, overcast.

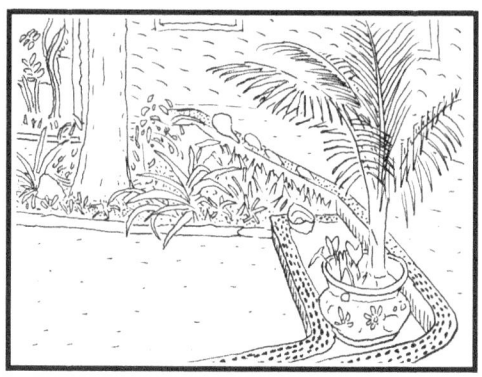

"Hotel Courtyard" p. 61
Holbox Island, Mexico
January, 2016, afternoon, mostly cloudy.

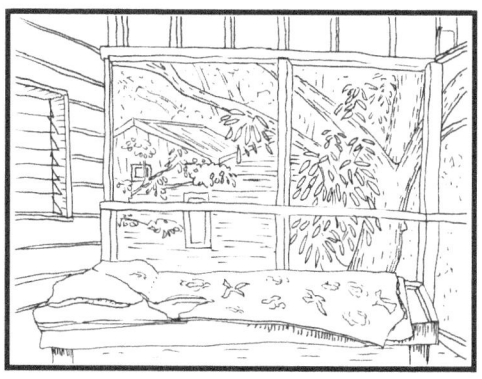

"Porch in the Trees" p. 65
Sittee River, Belize
January, late afternoon, sunny.

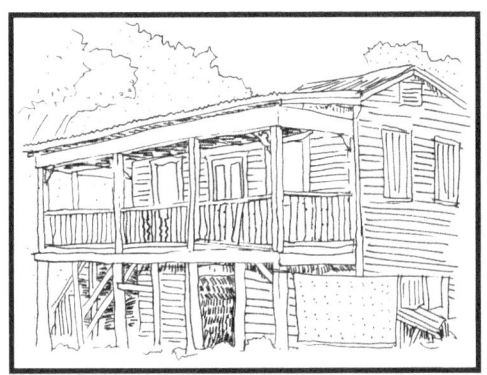

"Abandoned House" p. 69
Sittee River, Belize
January, early evening, low sun.
Old house, most likely damaged by floods over the years. Locals used one of its posts to secure a clothesline.

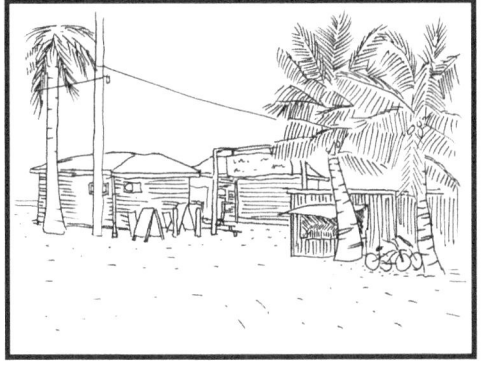

"Beach #3" p. 73
Caye Caulker, Belize
February, late morning, sunny.
This small narrow island in the Caribbean was broken in half by a hurricane. The channel left behind is known as "The Split". You're surrounded by ocean on three sides.

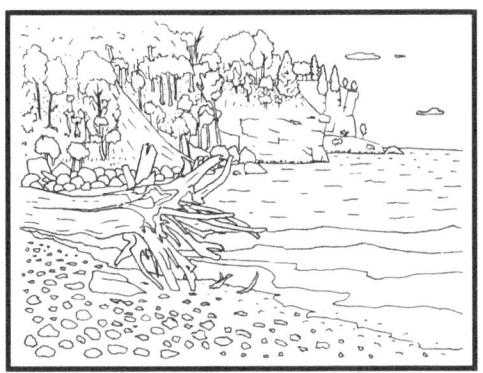

"Beach #4" p. 77
Lake Superior North Shore, Minnesota
May, midday, mostly sunny.
An isolated beach strewn with a dozen or more large, washed up trees. Perhaps they fell victim from a landslide just up the shore. When I returned a couple months later, they were all rearranged. The Great Lake making driftwood of grand proportions.

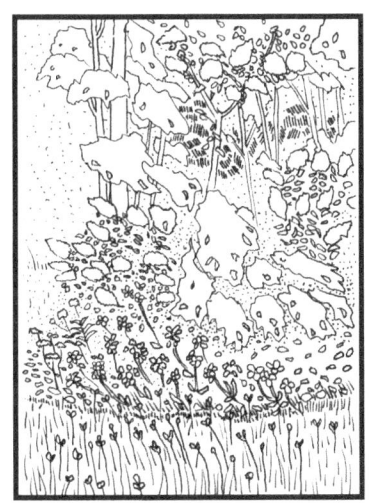

"Backyard" p. 81
Duluth, Minnesota
June, afternoon, sunny.
Lilacs, Dame's Rocket and Indian Paintbrush.

Also by C.C. Shepard

Relaxing Places: An Adult Coloring Book, Travel Size Edition

ISBN-10: 0-9983346-1-8
ISBN-13: 978-0-9983346-1-5

Available at www.ccshepardart.com and elsewhere online.

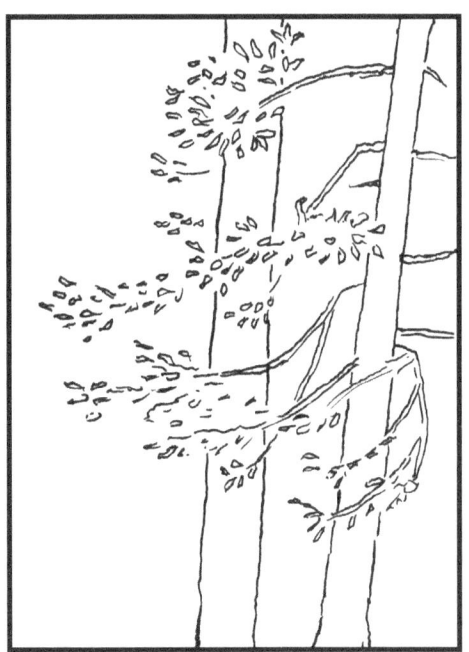

www.ingramcontent.com/pod-product-compliance
Lightning Source LLC
Chambersburg PA
CBHW080231180526

45158CB00010BA/3012